PENNSYLVANIA

Sarah Tieck

Published by ABDO Publishing Company, PO Box 398166, Minneapolis, MN 55439.

Printed in the United States of America, North Mankato, Minnesota.
052012
092012
♲ PRINTED ON RECYCLED PAPER

Coordinating Series Editor: Rochelle Baltzer
Contributing Editors: Megan M. Gunderson, BreAnn Rumsch, Marcia Zappa
Graphic Design: Adam Craven
Cover Photograph: *Shutterstock*: Caitlin Mirra.
Interior Photographs/Illustrations: *AP Photo*: AP Photo (p. 23), Pocono Record, Jason Farmer (p. 26), North Wind Picture Archives via AP Images (pp. 13, 23); *Getty Images*: Rob Carr (p. 27), Alan Levenson (p. 19), PBS Television/Courtesy of Getty Images (p. 25), Harry E. Walker/MCT/MCT via Getty Images (p. 21); *iStockphoto*: ©iStockphoto.com/aimintang (p. 27), ©iStockphoto.com/Davel5957 (p. 26), ©iStockphoto.com/drbueller (p. 5), ©iStockphoto.com/drnadig (p. 17), ©iStockphoto.com/Joesboy (p. 30), ©iStockphoto.com/sdominick (p. 27), ©iStockphoto.com/Terryfic3D (p. 19), ©iStockphoto.com/veni (p. 11); *Shutterstock*: Critterbiz (p. 30), Jeffrey M. Frank (p. 9), K. L. Kohn (p. 9), Philip Lange (p. 30), Caitlin Mirra (p. 29), Andrew Williams (p. 30).

All population figures taken from the 2010 US census.

Library of Congress Cataloging-in-Publication Data

Tieck, Sarah, 1976-
  Pennsylvania / Sarah Tieck.
    p. cm. -- (Explore the United States)
  ISBN 978-1-61783-376-2
  1. Pennsylvania--Juvenile literature. I. Title.
  F149.3.T54 2013
  974.8--dc23
                        2012016275

PENNSYLVANIA

Contents

ONE NATION

The United States is a **diverse** country. It has farmland, cities, coasts, and mountains. Its people come from many different backgrounds. And, its history covers more than 200 years.

Today the country includes 50 states. Pennsylvania is one of these states. Let's learn more about this state and its story!

Did You Know?

Pennsylvania became a state on December 12, 1787. It was the second state to join the nation.

Pennsylvania is home to important pieces from US history, such as the Liberty Bell.

Pennsylvania Up Close

The United States has four main **regions**. Pennsylvania is in the Northeast.

Pennsylvania has six states on its borders. New York is north. New Jersey is east. Delaware and Maryland are south. West Virginia is southwest. Ohio is west.

Pennsylvania has a total area of 46,055 square miles (119,282 sq km). About 12.7 million people live there.

Did You Know?

Washington DC is the US capital city. Puerto Rico is a US commonwealth. This means it is governed by its own people.

REGIONS OF THE UNITED STATES

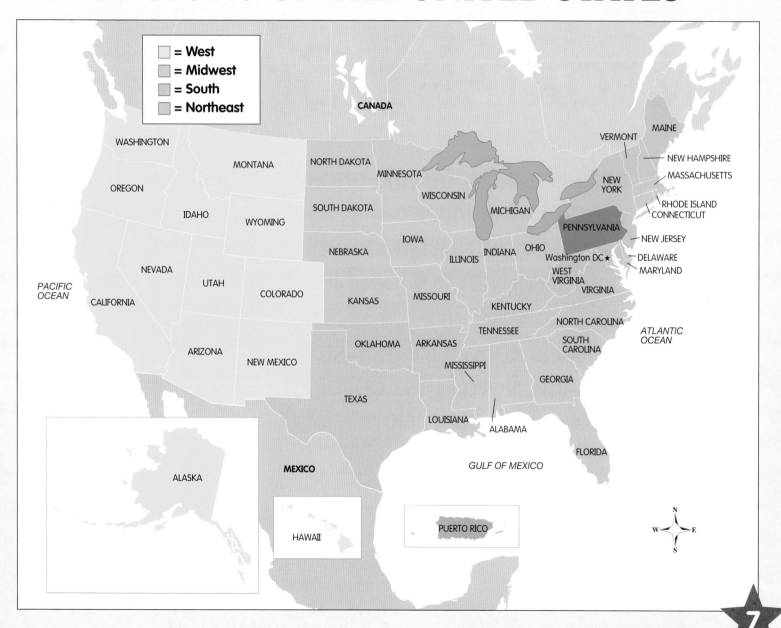

= West
= Midwest
= South
= Northeast

CANADA

WASHINGTON

MONTANA

OREGON

IDAHO

WYOMING

NORTH DAKOTA

MINNESOTA

SOUTH DAKOTA

WISCONSIN

MICHIGAN

IOWA

NEBRASKA

NEVADA

UTAH

COLORADO

KANSAS

MISSOURI

ILLINOIS

INDIANA

OHIO

Washington DC ★

WEST
VIRGINIA

VIRGINIA

KENTUCKY

PACIFIC
OCEAN

CALIFORNIA

VERMONT

MAINE

NEW HAMPSHIRE

MASSACHUSETTS

NEW
YORK

RHODE ISLAND
CONNECTICUT

PENNSYLVANIA

NEW JERSEY

DELAWARE

MARYLAND

ARIZONA

NEW MEXICO

OKLAHOMA

ARKANSAS

TENNESSEE

NORTH CAROLINA

SOUTH
CAROLINA

ATLANTIC
OCEAN

MISSISSIPPI

GEORGIA

TEXAS

LOUISIANA

ALABAMA

FLORIDA

ALASKA

MEXICO

GULF OF MEXICO

HAWAII

PUERTO RICO

N
W · E
S

IMPORTANT CITIES

Harrisburg is the **capital** of Pennsylvania. It is located on the Susquehanna River.

Philadelphia (fih-luh-DEHL-fee-uh) is the state's largest city. It is home to 1,526,006 people. It is an important US port on the Delaware River.

Philadelphia is known for its history. It was the first city in the state. And, it was the capital of the 13 colonies during the **Revolutionary War**.

Did You Know?

Philadelphia is nicknamed "Philly."

The Pennsylvania State Capitol is known for its green-tiled dome.

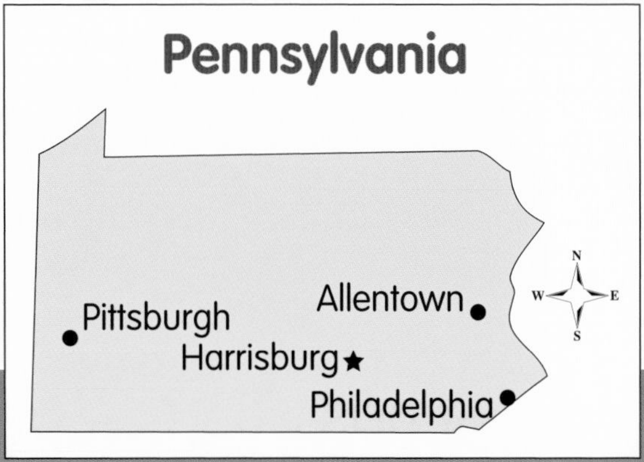

Pennsylvania

Pittsburgh

Allentown

Harrisburg ★

Philadelphia

N
W ✦ E
S

Philadelphia is home to many museums and historic places.

Did You Know?

The French and Indian War started in what is now Pittsburgh in 1754. The Ohio River was used for travel during the war.

Pittsburgh is Pennsylvania's second-largest city. It has 305,704 people. This city has a long history of making iron and steel.

Allentown is the third-largest city in the state. It is home to 118,032 people. This city has many manufacturing companies.

Two rivers meet in Pittsburgh to form the Ohio River.

Pennsylvania in History

Pennsylvania's history includes Native Americans and settlers. Native Americans were the first to live in what is now Pennsylvania. In 1681, Englishman William Penn started the colony of Pennsylvania.

By 1775, the colonists no longer wanted to be ruled by England. So that year, they began fighting in the **Revolutionary War**. They won in 1783. In 1787, Pennsylvania became the second state.

The Declaration of Independence was adopted at the State House in Philadelphia on July 4, 1776. Today, this building is called Independence Hall.

13

Timeline

1863

The Battle of Gettysburg took place near the town of Gettysburg. This **American Civil War** battle lasted three days. It was an important win for the North.

1775

American colonists began fighting in the **Revolutionary War**.

1790

Philadelphia became the US **capital**.

1700s

1800s

The US Constitution was written in Philadelphia. This important paper lists the basic US laws and rights.

The Johnstown floods killed more than 2,200 people. This was one of the state's worst disasters.

1787

1889

14

1903

Milton Hershey built a chocolate factory in what later became the community of Hershey.

1979

An accident occurred at a **nuclear** power plant at Three Mile Island. This made people more careful with nuclear power in the United States.

2011

A major blizzard hit parts of Pennsylvania and New York. Almost 15 inches (38 cm) of snow fell in Philadelphia!

1900s

2000s

Floods ruined parts of Pittsburgh and Johnstown.

1936

An airplane crashed in a field in Somerset County on September 11. This was part of the worst **terrorist** attack in US history.

2001

15

ACROSS THE LAND

Pennsylvania has forests, rivers, lakes, hills, valleys, and mountains. Lake Erie forms part of the state's northern border. The Susquehanna and the Ohio Rivers flow through the state.

Many types of animals make their homes in Pennsylvania. These include moles, muskrats, and black bears.

Did You Know?

In July, the average temperature in Pennsylvania is 71°F (22°C). In January, it is 27°F (-3°C).

The Pocono Mountains in northeastern
Pennsylvania are famous for their waterfalls.

EARNING A LIVING

Pennsylvania has important businesses. Many people have jobs helping visitors or working with the law. The state is also a top manufacturing state. Medicine, food, and steel are made there.

Pennsylvania has many natural **resources**. Its mines produce coal. Mushrooms and corn are two major crops grown in the state. Dairy products and livestock also come from the state's farms.

Steel made in Pennsylvania is used in cars, stoves, and knives.

The Hershey Company is located in the community of Hershey. It is North America's leading chocolate maker.

19

Sports Page

Pennsylvania is home to many **professional** sports teams. The Philadelphia Phillies and Pittsburgh Pirates play baseball. The Philadelphia Eagles and Pittsburgh Steelers play football.

College sports are also popular in the state. Pennsylvania State University, or Penn State, has a well-known football team.

As of 2012, the Steelers had more Super Bowl wins than any other team!

HOMETOWN HEROES

Many famous people are from Pennsylvania. James Buchanan was born near Mercersburg in 1791. He was the fifteenth US president. He served from 1857 to 1861.

Betsy Ross was born in Philadelphia in 1752. She sewed for a living. Many people believe she sewed the first American flag.

Buchanan was the US president in the years before the American Civil War started.

Many historians believe that Ross made the first US flag based on a drawing by George Washington.

23

Fred Rogers was born in Latrobe in 1928. Later he lived in Pittsburgh. He was a television star known to many as Mister Rogers.

Rogers is best known for *Mister Rogers' Neighborhood*. He wrote and hosted the popular children's show. He also wrote and sang songs for it. There were almost 1,000 **episodes** between 1968 and 2001!

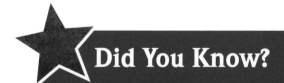

Did You Know?

Rogers received many honors and awards for his work. In 2002, he was given the Presidential Medal of Freedom.

24

Rogers was famous for changing into sneakers and a sweater during the show's opening song.

MISTER ROGERS' NEIGHBORHOOD

25

Tour Book

Do you want to go to Pennsylvania? If you visit the state, here are some places to go and things to do!

 ## Play

Go skiing or snowboarding in the Poconos! These mountains are a popular vacation spot.

 ## See

Visit Independence Hall in Philadelphia. The Declaration of Independence and the US Constitution were written inside this famous building.

★ Cheer

Catch a Little League baseball game! Every August, the Little League World Series is held in Williamsport.

★ Remember

Visit Gettysburg National Military Park. See where the Battle of Gettysburg happened. And, see where President Abraham Lincoln gave his famous speech, the Gettysburg Address.

★ Discover

Learn how chocolate is made at Hershey's Chocolate World in Hershey!

A Great State

The story of Pennsylvania is important to the United States. The people and places that make up this state offer something special to the country. Together with all the states, Pennsylvania helps make the United States great.

Lake Erie is one of Pennsylvania's natural wonders. It is a popular place for visitors. Also, it is useful to companies that ship goods.

Fast Facts

Date of Statehood:
December 12, 1787

Population (rank):
12,702,379
(6th most-populated state)

Total Area (rank):
46,055 square miles
(33rd largest state)

Motto:
"Virtue, Liberty, and
Independence"

Nickname:
Keystone State

State Capital:
Harrisburg

Flag:

Flower: Mountain Laurel

Postal Abbreviation:
PA

Tree: Eastern Hemlock

Bird: Ruffed Grouse

Important Words

American Civil War the war between the Northern and Southern states from 1861 to 1865.

capital a city where government leaders meet.

diverse made up of things that are different from each other.

episode one show in a series of shows.

nuclear a type of energy that uses atoms. Atoms are tiny particles that make up matter.

professional (pruh-FEHSH-nuhl) working for money rather than for pleasure.

region a large part of a country that is different from other parts.

resource a supply of something useful or valued.

Revolutionary War a war fought between England and the North American colonies from 1775 to 1783.

terrorist a person who uses violence to scare or control people or governments.

Web Sites

To learn more about Pennsylvania, visit ABDO Publishing Company online. Web sites about Pennsylvania are featured on our Book Links page. These links are routinely monitored and updated to provide the most current information available.

www.abdopublishing.com

Index